NUCLEUS

BY ALANA VALENTINE

CURRENCY PRESS
The performing arts publisher

GRIFFIN THEATRE COMPANY

CURRENT THEATRE SERIES

First published in 2025
by Currency Press Pty Ltd,
Gadigal Land, Suite 310, 46–56 Kippax Street, Surry Hills, NSW 2010, Australia
enquiries@currency.com.au
www.currency.com.au

in association with Griffin Theatre Company

Copyright: *Nucleus* © Alana Valentine, 2025.

COPYING FOR EDUCATIONAL PURPOSES

The Australian *Copyright Act 1968* [Act] allows a maximum of one chapter or 10% of this book, whichever is the greater, to be copied by any educational institution for its educational purposes provided that that educational institution [or the body that administers it] has given a remuneration notice to Copyright Agency [CA] under the Act. For details of the CA licence for educational institutions contact CA, 12 / 66 Goulburn Street, Sydney, NSW, 2000; tel: within Australia 1800 066 844 toll free; outside Australia 61 2 9394 7600; fax: 61 2 9394 7601; email: memberservices@copyright.com.au

Copying for Other Purposes

Except as permitted under the Act, for example a fair dealing for the purposes of study, research, criticism or review, no part of this book may be reproduced, stored in a retrieval system, or transmitted in any form or by any means without prior written permission. All enquiries should be made to the publisher at the address above.

No part of this book may be used or reproduced in any manner for the purpose of training artificial intelligence technologies or systems without the express written permission of the author and the publisher.

Any performance or public reading of *Nucleus* is forbidden unless a licence has been received from the author or the author's agent. The purchase of this book in no way gives the purchaser the right to perform the play in public, whether by means of a staged production or a reading. All applications for public performance should be addressed to the author c / - Creative Representation, PO Box 208, Surry Hills NSW 2010; tel 02 9690 5900; email admin@creativerep.com.au

Typeset by Brighton Gray for Currency Press.
Cover shows Paula Arundell; photo by Brett Boardman. Design by Susu Studio.

Currency Press acknowledges the Traditional Owners of the Country on which we live and work. We pay our respects to all Aboriginal and Torres Strait Islander Elders, past and present.

Contents

Nucleus 1

Theatre Program at the end of the playtext

Nucleus was first produced by Griffin Theatre Company at Seymour Centre, Gadigal Country, Sydney, on 14 February 2025, with the following cast:

   DR GABRIEL HULST   Peter Kowitz
   DR CASSIE LOGART   Paula Arundell

Director, Andrea James
Dramaturg, Dylan Van Den Berg
Set and Costume Designer, Isabel Hudson
Lighting Designer, Verity Hampson
Sound Designer, Phil Downing
Video Designer, Laura Turner
Stage Manager, Tanya Leach

Peter Kowitz and Paula Arundell in rehearsal (Photo: Brett Boardman)

Paula Arundell in rehearsal (Photo: Brett Boardman)

Alana Valentine in rehearsal (Photo: Brett Boardman)

Paula Arundell and Peter Kowitz in rehearsal (Photo: Brett Boardman)

CHARACTERS

DR GABRIEL HULST
DR CASSIE LOGART

NOTES

Although inspired in part by the truth of history and extensive research, this stage play is a fictional drama and does not depict any actual persons who are alive or dead.

The arrangement of continuous speech on separate lines and punctuation in the monologues is meant as a gentle guide for emphasis and pace (full stops and capitalization of words on a new line generally meaning a slight beat or slight emphasis). These may be observed but not act as any kind of impediment to interpretation of how the line is performed. Words without capitals but on a new line may indicate an even slighter shift but, again, only be used as a gentle guide rather than a prescriptive rule.

SETTING

A dream. A memory. A bar. A pool. A room.

This playtext went to press before the end of rehearsals and may differ from the play as performed.

Paula Arundell in rehearsal (Photo: Brett Boardman)

1.

GABRIEL: Cassie Logart is just so dishonest.
    I'm sorry, but it's difficult for me to express how much I dislike Cassie Logart's opinion.
    I've known her since the seventies.
    She's the anti-nuclear objector who said that a uranium enrichment plant in the Spencer Gulf would contaminate the Great Artesian Basin.
    Which is absolute rubbish.
    Spencer Gulf is nowhere near the Great Artesian Basin.

Cassie Logart has no credibility whatsoever. I am currently on the advisory committee … I mean, I'm not actually taking any meetings but I am part of the advocacy lobby. So you may be surprised to know that it is Cassie Logart who prompted me to speak today and tell you what happened around nuclear power in Australia from my point of view. I would ask you please not to judge before you hear me out, but also know that what I reveal to you today should not disqualify any opinions I have about the viability of nuclear power.

Time to take a long drink of water, Cassie.
    You see mine here is slightly cloudy.
    Not as bad as Adelaide tap water. This will eventually settle.
    Adelaide water would stay cloudy for the duration.

Let's begin with the fact that the science is not contestable.
    Science is not about opinion or argument.
    There's no doubt about what happens scientifically in a nuclear reactor.
    People talk about waste but nobody asks that about wind farms.
    Why ask it about a nuclear reactor?
    I'm just saying that the waste from wind farms is also very toxic.
    Cassie Logart said that the Chernobyl nuclear accident caused this huge number of abortions and she says it as though it was a direct result of the radioactive leakage from the reactor.

In fact, the abortions were carried out by physicians who were advising the women that they were going to have deformed babies. But she doesn't explain that. That's why I don't regard her as having any credibility.

I am a qualified nuclear engineer who has studied the biological effects of radiation.

    And I'm telling you, no-one takes Doctor Logart seriously.

    I am a fellow of the Institute of Engineers.

    Fellow means something better than member.

    I am also a Fellow of the Australasian Radiation Protection Society.

    There are several people who have similar qualifications.

    If Cassie Logart came to a meeting of the Australasian Radiation Protection Society, they'd never let her in, but if they did she would be laughed out of the room.

    Nobody takes her seriously.

    Are there any anti-nuclear people in the ARPS?

    Yes, there are.

    In fact it worries me how many are anti-nuclear.

    But they are not utter *meshuggener* like she is.

The whole of my career was working in this business.

    My degree in engineering was at Delft University of Technology in the Netherlands.

    You may have heard of it?

    And, just briefly, my father was the works manager and later on the director of a small company making chemicals in the south of the Netherlands.

    For Roche in Switzerland.

    I did odd jobs in the factory at times.

    I have an older brother. He's dead now. He went into agriculture. Not very successfully I'm afraid.

    When I was at school I was interested in science.

    I was good at everything; I hate to put it that way but I was very bright.

I did need to work for a scholarship but I got it, so I enrolled to do a PhD. In our final year we were expected to go and get a job in industry, and when we'd done that a few times we were permitted to apply for a vacation job. I chose Shell in France and then Seeber in Basel.

I had a week before my final return ticket was due. So I holidayed in Switzerland. And I met an Australian girl in the Alps, in the upper reaches of the Reichenbach Falls, made famous as the place where the fictional detective Sherlock Holmes vanquished his foe, Professor Moriarty. So that's how I finished up in Australia: I married an Australian girl.

One of my early-career jobs was to advise the British government about their plans to build a nuclear-powered merchant vessel.

I had to advise them that in all honesty it was not a good idea.

Economically, it didn't stack up.

Nowadays, small reactors are being developed but in those days reactors were much bigger and just not economical to put on a merchant ship.

So I told the British government, 'don't waste your money.'

[*As govt official*] 'You realise you've talked yourself out of a job.'

'Yes,' I said. 'Give me a couple of days and I can probably talk them out of yours.'

At that time the chief engineer from the Australian Atomic Energy Commission happened to be visiting the researchers where I was working in the UK, and I think he heard about this joke and I managed to get an interview with him. He offered me a job working for what was then called the Australian Atomic Energy Commission. Established at Lucas Heights, where you have Australia's only nuclear facility. Later on they changed the acronym to ANSTO. Australian Nuclear Science and Technology Organisation. I was taken on to look at the possible applications of nuclear power in Australia.

It meant living in Sydney, but it was still a very attractive proposition.

1.2

CASSIE: Would you like to play?
GABRIEL: What?
CASSIE: Pick a card, any card.

She holds out a deck of cards. He reluctantly chooses.

So now you act out the symptoms and we guess which it is.
GABRIEL: It says zero-point-seven to ten Gy.
CASSIE: No. You can't tell us. That's the level of radiation. The correct answer is bone marrow degeneration and you have to show us the symptoms.
GABRIEL: I'm not good at games.
CASSIE: Pick again. Come on, you came to gloat. I mean, visit. You may as well play.

He reluctantly picks another card.

Now don't tell us. Act out the symptoms.

GABRIEL *mimes weakness, fatigue, fainting, confusion.*

No. Let me guess. Fainting. Confusion.

GABRIEL *mimes hair loss.*

Hair loss.

GABRIEL *mimes vomiting.*

Nausea and vomiting.
GABRIEL: What is this?
CASSIE: It's fallout bingo.
GABRIEL: I'm not playing this game with you, Cassie.
CASSIE: Well, you are, Gabriel. You're playing it with the planet which, for the next little while at least, still has me on it.
GABRIEL: You're a crank.
CASSIE: I'm a doctor. And I'm going to guess in excess of fifty Gy and neurovascular degeneration.
GABRIEL: Bingo. What does one win?
CASSIE: The right to say I told you so.
GABRIEL: [*to the audience*] Did I tell you so? You see why I didn't even want to come here.

CASSIE: You should have mimed bleeding from the anus and ulcers in the mouth, and the sloughing off of skin. We had one woman here who mimed peeling off the skin with such immaculate accuracy. It was amazing. Started at the top of the arm and just peeled the skin down and down and down. She was a regular Marcel Marceau.

1.3

He sighs. Then goes on.

GABRIEL: I have two children. Lucy, and Gerry, he has a catering company in Melbourne. Gerry was born in 1966 and then in 1969 Lucy was born.

When we got to Australia, these things were happening.
 Australia was interested in building enrichment plants to enrich uranium. One of my colleagues was put in charge of developing a centrifuge enrichment process.
 At that stage the chairman of the Australian Atomic Energy Commission in Australia was Sir Phillip Baxter, who was the vice-chancellor of the University of NSW and a chemical engineer.
 Also, he secretly wanted to build a bomb.
 He wanted to have the option of building a bomb.
 So, it was useful for him to have a natural uranium reactor to create plutonium, which is used to make bombs.
 There's two ways to make a bomb. One way is to use natural uranium and bleed plutonium from it, and the other way is to breed it from enriched uranium.
 The much easier way is to make plutonium from natural uranium.

The other thing was that they wanted a nuclear power station.
 Gorton was Prime Minister.
 Gorton got the job when Harold Holt drowned. Disappeared at sea. Maybe he drowned, maybe a submarine came and got him. In any case he ceased to be Prime Minister and Gorton took over.
 And Gorton was very much in favour of having a nuclear power station at Jervis Bay.
 It was decided that I would be employed to investigate and clear the site.

Jervis Bay was chosen because it was Commonwealth Territory so they didn't have to kowtow to the NSW government. In Jervis Bay the Commonwealth could, and still can, make decisions without the approval of NSW. Lucas Heights is Commonwealth property, Jervis Bay is Commonwealth Territory.

So, it was all green lights.

All ready to go.

We cleared the way for the ocean outfall for the cooling water. It was designed so that it would bring in cooling water from the ocean, and then after it had gone through the reactor, the water would be discharged into the bay. Because cooling water is used to condense the steam after it has been through the turbine.

Then we investigated the potential for earthquakes. If you look at the south head of Jervis Bay, Point Perpendicular, it looks like a fault line. But it's got nothing to do with earthquakes. Certainly that was part of the environmental investigation.

It was concluded that seismic was not a problem and Australia was considered not to have any seismic risk at all. Possibly because they didn't know much about it. There was an earthquake engineering committee set up in the mid-seventies, ANCEE, and we now know that Australia does have seismic vulnerabilities. But Jervis Bay was not considered to be a seismic risk.

So the next thing I got involved with was calling for tenders, internationally, to build the reactor.

I was part of the team overseeing which reactor we should buy.

1969, the site was cleared, the ocean outfall outlet was installed, and tenders were in. One from Canada, one from America, one from Westinghouse and a German company that doesn't exist anymore, and one from the British.

But no tender was ever awarded.

Because silly Billy McMahon went and cancelled the whole thing.

That's all it took.

Change of a Prime Minister.

Malcolm Fraser denounced Gorton and resigned from cabinet.

McMahon became PM.

He'd been Minister for External Affairs, what we now call Foreign Minister, and he encouraged the government to sign the Nuclear Non-Proliferation Treaty in 1970.

So the first thing he did, the moment after he shook hands with the Governor General, Big-Ears McMahon put the kibosh on the whole kit and kaboodle.

He's seen as a bit of a joke of a PM, a footnote in Liberal history, the bottom of the barrel after twenty-two years of Liberal rule.

He was the one who stopped Australia getting a nuclear power plant that could have generated weapons-grade plutonium.

You won't find many protesters who can talk about that time.

Some of them have passed on of course, and some have lost their marbles.

Might find someone who built the road out to Murrays Beach. The road to nowhere as it turned out.

There was a bit of local agitation.

As far as I can calculate, Cassie's mother dragged her out there as a teenager. She was a housewife crusader so Cassie inherited the family business.

It was nothing like what you'd see later.

Not the protest movements of the eighties where Cassie Logart flourished into a protest celebrity. No, what stopped it was not protest.

It was the Right Honourable Sir William McMahon.

I took part in a handing-back ceremony. The site was part of the National Parks and it had been handed to us to build the reactor and so, we handed it back. To the National Parks Authority.

And … I …

Pause.

I …

He sighs.

I have always been very interested in the biological effects of radiation.

If there's an accident.

That's what worries most people.

What could go wrong and the consequences if the radiation gets out.

As an engineer I can work myself ragged to make sure nothing does go wrong, but I also need to know what happens if the engineering fails.

So I researched it for many years, ten years, and I made findings.

So I did what scientists do: I went to a conference to present my findings.

To the International Commission on Radiological Protection.

I gave my paper about the biological effects of radiation.

And what I said was that radiation can be quite beneficial to health in low doses.

That my scientific opinion is that it is not as consequential if humans are exposed to radiation as people may think.

That there is a whole industry devoted to scare mongering about the negative effects of radiation

I was happy to be provocative.

Because nonsense about the biological effects of radiation was the reason why all that work I had done, all that energy I had expended, came to nothing.

I thought I would just move on, and that is what I did but I never liked, I still don't like, the ways in which science is distorted by people with dishonest agendas.

So I gave my paper and afterwards I did something else that I very rarely do.

I went to the conference bar, the White Orchid bar.

I knew that there were LNT fanatics there but I don't know, on this night, you might say I was looking for a fight.

You know what LNT is? Linear No-Threshold.

It's a working theory that the risk of radiation is proportional to the dose without a threshold. Basically it assumes that every increment of radiation dose, no matter how small, constitutes an increased cancer risk for humans. And that if you plot risk on one side and dose on the other there is a linear relationship right back to zero. But everyone with a science degree knows that it's not back to zero, it's more complicated, and there is a threshold where it is actually beneficial. Everyone knows that LNT is not true. Except Cassie Logart. More likely she knows it's not true but she chooses to lie about it.

But you want to know about the bar and whether I got into a fight.

Well, I didn't get into a fight because a woman in the bar smiled at me.

We were in a room full of young people, mostly students, and this very attractive woman smiled at me.

And women do not smile at me in that way.

But she did.

And so I did what was biologically predictable.

I went over to her

And she kept smiling and laughing and I was drinking and she had seen me give my paper and she was flattering me and asking very astute questions and I guess it was a vulnerable moment for me.

Because we did what was biologically predictable.

And that was how I first met Cassie Logart.

Who I believe deliberately targeted me because of my opposing … stance.

And who now could actually—very effectively, without ever even saying anything or threatening me in any way—silence me from speaking out any further about my findings.

I didn't know that yet.

We parted and both made some joke about what happens at conferences stays at conferences.

It was a very nice night

And I'm not particularly experienced

So for me it was about variety

I had met and married my wife and had very little

Experience

To be clear

I didn't know who she was.

2.

CASSIE: I knew who he was.
 I seduced him knowing who he was.
 I'd seen him give his speech.
 I knew he was married.
 He was wearing his wedding ring in the bar.
 I don't like the phrase 'honey trap'
 It's just so degrading, as if my vagina doesn't have an equivalent say in the proceedings
 I mean, come on.
 That is a fun fantasy isn't it?
 Doing it for a cause erotique.
 Look, it wasn't that calculated, really.
 I wasn't Cassie Logart yet.
 I mean, I had been active, I was committed
 But people weren't listening.
 Were not listening to little old me
 So I saw an opportunity to fuck him in more ways than one and I took it.
 It's hard for the women we become to understand the girls we were.
 I look back and I see beauty traded for power.
 My plan was to write some sort of article for a student paper. What did I think that would do? It was the eighties, casual sex was quotidian, but a scandal could still take someone out of the game. A stain, a lapse of judgement, a mistake that could follow him. My strategy was to use what I had to get what I wanted.
 Because even then I knew that the entire pro-nuclear position is a lie.
 The idea that nuclear energy is clean energy is a whopper.
 Why?
 Because, to enrich uranium—it mostly has to be enriched to be able to use in reactors—to do that, you need a huge amount of energy which is produced by coal.
 So, you have to dig up the uranium using diesel-fuelled vehicles and diesel-fuelled digging equipment.

Then, once you have transported it using fossil fuels and safeguarded it in containers made by fossil fuels, then you have to build the reactor.

Making concrete provides a thirty percent increase in CO_2.

And then how long does a nuclear power plant last?

Not forever, not by a long shot.

Twenty years, forty at most.

Then you have to decommission it and cut it apart and you have to take the waste and store it away for half a million years.

And if it leaks, if it escapes, if it goes into the water supply and the food chain, which is inevitable, do you want me to tell you what it does to children?

Because I can tell you.

I can describe their deformities, do you want me to go on?

So to say nuclear energy is clean and green is not just a lie, it is the worst possible lie.

It is a lie that would destroy all life on this planet.

Not maybe

I am a paediatrician, and I can tell you what radioactivity does to children.

It deforms them.

Have I used questionable tactics?

No more questionable than their side has.

Could you call some of the things I have said contestable?

Perhaps, but only if you call all of the things they say lies.

And, you know the science itself is not contestable.

I am a scientist. I'm a doctor and the biological effects of radiation are appalling.

Appalling to human life.

And he was saying the opposite.

Listen.

My boyfriend was hedging his bets

[*As her boyfriend*] 'I only said I wanted an open relationship'

[*Whispering*] So when I picked up and slept with Doctor Gabriel Hulst it wasn't Machiavellian

It was filthy bad so it was a huge turn-on

It was so wrong, so WRONG
Every moment of it I knew it was a terrible thing to do
To him, to myself, to his credibility, to my cause
I mean, it was so WRONG that I don't think I have ever come to orgasm
so fast and so fully ever in my life before
The sex was
Memorable.
Memorable.
Bloody hell
Because he was him, I wasn't me
Do you know what I mean? I mean, he was the devil, the man who wanted to put a nuclear reactor on the headland and he had no idea who I was
And now he was compromised
So compromised
And it was too good to be true
And too bad to be good
And it was the end of his life
If I wanted it to be
And the only fly in the ointment
was
no, not love
I mean the sex was memorable and he really was very nice
Disarmingly nice
No, the thing was, when I realised
That he made some very persuasive arguments about nuclear power.
Very persuasive scientific points about it
And for a moment I thought I was actually in danger
Not seriously, not seriously, for a moment
But here's the thing: I had to listen as part of the ruse
I had to consider the possibility and I had to find ways to respond and
I dunno.
They say that if we can but pretend to be kind
Eventually we will become kind
If we can but pretend to be happy

We will be happy
Well, I guess the years put that one to bed
Anyway, I took his argument out for a walk, that's all, and then I soon got over it

The other thing that made the encounter linger of course was the pregnancy

Stops.

I couldn't very well get rid of it
Because I wanted a baby and I thought this one might get my boyfriend to pop the question and in truth of fact it did
And my husband never knew that the child was not his
And the enemy never knew that the child was his
And the child never knew who her real father was
And I wondered how I would deal with it if she questioned my entire position on nuclear power and decided, as a provocation to me, that she would take a job as a nuclear power advocate.
And that *was* a hard day
Knowing what I knew about her genome
I mean, opinion is nurture not nature
But I couldn't help wonder if there was something in it
I mean, wouldn't you wonder if you'd made a mistake like that?

3.

GABRIEL: So when I made the worst mistake of my life
I didn't know it was the worst mistake
Until several months later
I was down in Adelaide to consult with politicians about the business possibilities of nuclear fuel cycle waste management.
This was many years before the Royal Commission.
South Australia had been flirting with the idea of nuclear waste disposal management for many years.
And so they should.
All that empty desert, it's the perfect place to store it.
And if you engineer the containers well it will not escape into the environment.

It won't.

France stores its own nuclear waste and that doesn't stop you going to Paris on holidays, does it?

There's a spent nuclear fuel repository in Finland where they bury the waste in deep, deep caverns on the west coast, near the Olkiluoto Nuclear Power Plant.

It's brilliant.

And there's no environmental impact.

Do you know that Cassie Logart actually told the Royal Commission—I'm talking about more recently—she told them that twenty-five percent of all cancers are due to radiation exposure.

Which is insane.

I spoke to her afterwards and I said that is not a fact, that is just your estimate.

CASSIE: Yes, that is just my estimate, but I was speaking for myself.

GABRIEL: But everyone knows that she is a liar. All medical people know that she uses tactics that are just … execrable.

But I'm telling you about the first time I knew who she was

maybe three months after we briefly got together at the conference.

I was going into Parliament House in Adelaide and there was a small group of anti-nuclear protestors on the steps.

And there she was.

Holding one of those posters—'No Nukes is good nukes'—and a big red cross in the centre.

And when I saw her it was like a uranium nucleus was splitting inside my head.

Oh yes, it's the nucleus that splits.

All very well to say it splits the atom.

It does, but more specifically it splits the nucleus.

That's why it's called nuclear energy.

CASSIE: Some people do call it atomic energy.

GABRIEL: Listen, I don't want to have to explain fission to you but just for you to understand who I am and how I think and how utterly wonderful nuclear science is, I will very simply and briefly say that the process accelerates a neutron which strikes a target nucleus, usually Uranium-235.

This strike splits the nucleus of the uranium atom, breaking it down into two isotopes, three high speed neutrons and a lot of energy.
    A payload, a plenitude, really, a seriously gargantuan
    utterly humungous fuckload of energy

I know you wouldn't expect me to swear in that way but there really is no other adjective that appropriately describes the amount of energy released.

The wonder of uranium as an element is that it is fissile, meaning as you will deduce, that it will decay over time.
    Yes, uranium is breaking down, in nature we are talking between one hundred and fifty thousand years and four-point-five billion years.

What we do in a nuclear reactor is simply speed up the process of nature.

Now I know that I am using science and my fascination with science to divert from the moment when I saw Cassie Logart on the protest line and I understood what had been done to me.
    I do that.

CASSIE: We do that.

GABRIEL: Everything you see around you has been designed by engineers for efficiency, practicality, durability.
    We are the authors of modernity.
    What is the difference between two centuries ago and now?
    The genius of brilliant engineering.
    Simple as that.
    So.
    Simple as that I saw her in the protest gaggle.
    I told no-one about it for weeks.
    Months.
    It wasn't guilt
    It was that I didn't want to have a life with someone who I couldn't tell everything to.
    That's why people tell their spouses, you know
    Not because of the rewards of being honest

Because you feel the loss of not being able to tell your wife, who you love,
Everything that is going on with you
So that's what I decided to do
Eventually
I decided that I would tell my wife
Because I wanted to be able to speak publicly about the positive benefits of nuclear power and I didn't want Cassie Logart to have that hold over me.
My wife forgave me, which she shouldn't have done.
I never strayed again, I can tell you that.
But it was still a terrible mistake because I never stopped thinking about her.

4.

A bar. Painted with white orchids.

CASSIE: Do you have a mini bar in your room?
GABRIEL: Yes. All the rooms have them.

> *Pause.*

I've often wondered what an alcoholic does when they go into the room they have paid to sleep in and it is stocked with their living fear.
CASSIE: Let's not think about abstinence.
GABRIEL: Why did you ask about the bar then?
CASSIE: I'd like another drink.
GABRIEL: I'll get you one.
CASSIE: In your room.

> *Pause.*

GABRIEL: No, that's not a good idea.
CASSIE: It's my idea.
GABRIEL: Yes, but you have had a drink and your ideas may be muddled.
CASSIE: You don't find me attractive?
GABRIEL: I hadn't thought about it.

> *Pause.*

CASSIE: Then think about it now.

GABRIEL: I've made commitments. Vows. It's too much of a cliché for me to have a convention romance.
CASSIE: You consider yourself better than that?
GABRIEL: I suppose I do.
CASSIE: Have you enjoyed our conversation?
GABRIEL: Yes. Very much.
CASSIE: So you see for me going upstairs and being in bed and being intimate, it's all just an extension of the conversation. It's not this big thing that others make it.
GABRIEL: Well that may be so.
CASSIE: But it is still a big thing for you.
GABRIEL: Of course.
CASSIE: Your time is your own, your voice is your own, your mind is your own but your body is not.
GABRIEL: Technically. No.
CASSIE: And does that work for you?
GABRIEL: How do you mean?
CASSIE: Attraction is chemical. Biological. It's not moral.
GABRIEL: Of course.
CASSIE: Purely scientifically I can mean nothing to you but want to kiss you.
GABRIEL: So it seems.

She leans forward and kisses him.

CASSIE: You can't observe the femme without wanting to see the fatale.
GABRIEL: I can.
CASSIE: You haven't been with many women.
GABRIEL: You can't know that.

CASSIE looks at him.

CASSIE: What if I just gave you a massage?
GABRIEL: But you won't just give me a massage.
CASSIE: Of course I won't.
GABRIEL: No.
CASSIE: If you had slept with women before your wife, do you consider them a betrayal?
GABRIEL: No, of course I did.
CASSIE: But not many. Not a big variety.

GABRIEL: Enough.
CASSIE: Not really.
GABRIEL: Sufficient to my needs.
CASSIE: But you're a curious person. Not just common or garden variety curious. Deeply curious. About all areas of life, except physical pleasure.
GABRIEL: Well that's true.
CASSIE: So is there a way you could consider it research?
GABRIEL: You're not serious?
CASSIE: I'm not. I'm just giving you time to change your mind.
GABRIEL: I'm not going to change my mind.
CASSIE: Okay.

Pause.

GABRIEL: You feel confident in more physical conversations?
CASSIE: I do.
GABRIEL: Why is that?
CASSIE: Well, I know how you abhor the cliché so let's forget it.
GABRIEL: Please. Go on.
CASSIE: My father never rated me, ever. He always corrected me, always knew better than me, always had a more elaborate opinion, a more informed position. When I achieved anything, it was a lucky break; when I didn't, it was a lesson to learn my place. I got his approval, as many girls do, by being attractive. Oh, it was nothing creepy, nothing in the least ambiguous. It was just that I learned to be expressive with my touch, with my … skin. That sounds dodgy but it wasn't at all. It was … we have five senses that's all—taste, touch, smell, sight and sound. Conversation is sight and sound. What I'd like to know is your taste, touch and smell.
GABRIEL: I can understand that.
CASSIE: Well, I've talked too much.
GABRIEL: No … I … What if instead of the mini bar, I showed you something in the bathroom?
CASSIE: Ah … why?

Pause.

GABRIEL: Most people, as you say, are drawn to the mechanics of the mini bar, its little screw-top bottles. And you may think that the little screw caps in the bathroom are basically the same. Take off the cap, out comes the liquid. But for the liquid in the shampoo or the conditioner or any number of other things to come out of the tube, it requires a knowledge of physics. To make it squeeze, so to speak.

Pause.

CASSIE: Just how weird are you, Gabriel?

GABRIEL: Not in the least weird. Curious, in a way that it seems you are too.

CASSIE: Curious. It's our point of consensus.

GABRIEL: Well, our point of confluence, at least.

5.

CASSIE: I haven't told you something
    There's something I skipped over
    that morning after I met Gabriel
    Because I did know who he was and I did think it was a bit of a joke
    Maybe more
    And I talked about the sex because, well, because you always get attention and approval for talking about enjoying sex
    If you're a woman, nothing more certain
    Him against me, and I talk about how good the sex was, you're with me.
    But all that
    All that is just surface
    'I knew who he was'
    'I wanted to fuck him this way and that'
    Women get rewarded for swagger too
    Strategic swagger, femme fatale boasting
    Yeah, I know what he wants to do to the world
    How insanely stupid nuclear power is, insanely stupid.
    But what I haven't told you
    What I have barely …

Stops.

We went down to breakfast. I knew that if we were seen together at breakfast that was good, that could be good to prove it had happened beyond taking my word for it … but then

There was no-one there for breakfast

We were late

There was the waitress so that was still mission accomplished

But then out of his pocket he pulled this little shampoo bottle from the hotel room

And he pushed this little shampoo bottle across to me and he said, 'When you are disillusioned about life, when you feel a sense of disappointment and pain about what life can anymore offer, a staleness of engagement, a temporary loss of inspiration and enjoyment, let me suggest this.

Go to the bathroom and really look at the way this little bottle has been engineered.'

And in that moment

I can't describe it

I just wondered if it was possible to love someone with whom you disagreed utterly?

Utterly.

I knew he was married but men have left their wives before now

Madness

Utter madness because of some little moment with a shampoo bottle

And it wasn't just the bottle of course, it was the man

The sincerity of the man

Who could never imagine that someone might seduce him to destroy him

He looked at me and the little tube, smiling, and I thought, I don't really want to hurt you now.

I

Stops

I pulled myself together.

Later.

And I never made it public, or told his wife,

And I just acted as if it never happened
Later when I was more well known
I used to stand and talk about nuclear armageddon and I'd be thinking, now does this wooden podium deflect bullets? I was prepared to die. I would see someone stand up to ask me a question with a lump in their pocket and I would rush off the stage.

I met the cellist Jacqueline du Pré and she told me that when she was travelling she was so lonely, she'd put her cello up in a chair next to her. So. When she played she got adulation, but all the rest of the time she was lonely. And that was me too.

When I was out on the anti-nuclear talk circuit.
 I never doubted why I was doing it; I knew why, but it was lonely.
 I could never have imagined that my life would be in and out of bathrooms with all these pesky little bottles.

I always knew how to persuade. I'm just that sort of person. I was like that since I was a little girl.
 I decided when I was nine that I was going to be a doctor.
 Some people say I stopped nuclear war and I may well have. After I visited the American President he started saying that nuclear war must never be fought because it could never be won. Just after I visited him. I don't know if it was just me. How do we know what we have achieved if you are living your passion?
 I knew how to get a media profile
 and people listened to me
 But then my husband named a spider after me.
 I'd been away somewhere. Another conference.

I gave a great speech. I came back from the trip and it was my birthday. And my husband had Trudy in the car. He met me at the airport and he gave me a hug and said,

[*As her husband*] 'I have to tell you something.'
 [*As herself*] And I said, 'what?'
 And he said,
 [*As her husband*] 'I can't tell you now. We need to wait till we get home.'
 So we got home and we went into the bedroom and I said, 'what?'

And he said,

[*As her husband*] 'I've decided to sponsor a spider at Taronga Park and I called it after you.'

And then we went on for a couple of days and we were all having dinner around our lovely wooden table. And I said, 'Dad's got something to tell you' and he said

[*As her husband*] 'I've decided to sponsor a spider and name it after Mum.'

Then he changed the subject.

Trudy said something obscure about tangled webs but I was clueless.

He didn't tell me about the other woman for two weeks.

Then he said

[*As her husband*] 'I've been seeing another woman.'

I was strangely unaffected.

I even thought it was a good idea.

But I found out where the other woman lived and I just went and sat outside her apartment, in the hallway.

I knocked on the door and told her who I was and she refused to let me in.

I didn't want to go in.

I wanted to sit in the corridor, so I did.

She called the police and they came and told me I couldn't sit there.

'She's having an affair with my husband,' I told them.

'Even so, you have to go home.'

6.

The indoor pool of a large hotel. GABRIEL *and* CASSIE *are in swimming costumes.*

CASSIE: Gabriel?
GABRIEL: No.
CASSIE: I was just going to use the hotel pool.
GABRIEL: Please don't speak to me.
CASSIE: Fine.
GABRIEL: What are you doing here?
CASSIE: I'm staying here.

GABRIEL: Deliberately? Staying at this hotel. Came down to use the pool when you knew I'd be here?
CASSIE: Of course not. Can you calm down?
GABRIEL: Don't tell me to calm down.
CASSIE: I'm just saying, the sun is barely up and I just came down to have a quiet morning swim.
GABRIEL: Is that what you tell yourself?
CASSIE: Gabriel. This is paranoia.
GABRIEL: This is revelation.
CASSIE: I have never mentioned it to a soul.
GABRIEL: Haven't you boasted about it? To your rabble?
CASSIE: I never have.
GABRIEL: Of course you did. Everything you do is done with total calculation.
CASSIE: You don't know me.
GABRIEL: No. I don't want to know you. Ever. Ever. If I never see you again that will be too soon.
CASSIE: Calm down.
GABRIEL: If you were dying, alone, I wouldn't spit on your grave.
CASSIE: Hey angry man. Stop making choices and then blaming me.

Pause.

GABRIEL: I apologise.
CASSIE: Accepted.
GABRIEL: Just tell me. Did you specifically target me or was I just a random choice?
CASSIE: It was three years ago.
GABRIEL: I asked you a question.
CASSIE: And I decline to discuss it.
GABRIEL: That's a funny kind of apology.
CASSIE: That is not an apology.
GABRIEL: That much I can agree with.
CASSIE: I came down to use the pool. I am staying in the same hotel. That's going to happen Gabriel. We are in the same world.
GABRIEL: We are not even remotely on the same planet. You came here to harass and disrupt our IAEA sessions. You are here as a spoiler, Cassie.

CASSIE: I came here because a friend of mine is getting married. She left her husband for her ex-lover and her friends have deserted her. Except me.
GABRIEL: Saviour of all womankind.
CASSIE: Go swallow strontium chloride, cracker.

Pause. GABRIEL *shakes his head.*

GABRIEL: Only you.
CASSIE: What?
GABRIEL: Anyone else would have told me to shove it up my arse or go soak my head. Only you would abuse me with a chemically literate slur.
CASSIE: Strontium choride burns red, making it perfect for fireworks.

Pause. He smiles, despite himself.

GABRIEL: The story about your friend leaving her husband.
CASSIE: It's not a story.
GABRIEL: Childhood sweetheart?
CASSIE: Someone she picked up at a conference.
GABRIEL: Not really.
CASSIE: Not really.
GABRIEL: That doesn't happen in real life.
CASSIE: Not in your kind of half-life, no.
GABRIEL: People have to share values to be able to share a life.
CASSIE: Yes.
GABRIEL: What you value, what you believe, what you have faith in is the only basis for …
CASSIE: For what?
GABRIEL: For anything.

Pause.

CASSIE: It's early. I really was just coming down here to swim.
GABRIEL: Please.
CASSIE: Shared values. That's your theory on love.
GABRIEL: You're the only one mentioning love.
CASSIE: Yes. I guess I am.

Pause.

GABRIEL: Deeper than values is character, propensity and perhaps some kind of chemical effect.

CASSIE: At our core?
GABRIEL: [*leans close to her*] It wasn't me, it wasn't the thrill. It was not being yourself for a night, for a time.
CASSIE: You saw that?
GABRIEL: That's you.
CASSIE: Shall I tell you what I saw?
GABRIEL: No.
CASSIE: I saw a man with whom I can have hard conversations.
GABRIEL: Stop looking at me.
CASSIE: A man who really wants to know.
GABRIEL: Stop seeing me.
CASSIE: Why?
GABRIEL: It's easier for both of us if we just ... don't look.

7.

CASSIE *is alone on stage, playing cards. She uses a water jug to pour a glass of water and take two tablets from a small bottle in her pocket.*

GABRIEL *enters and looks around.*

GABRIEL: I thought I was coming to your workplace.
CASSIE: Keep up.
GABRIEL: How long has it been?
CASSIE: You think I've been sitting here, counting the years?
GABRIEL: I didn't say that.
CASSIE: Several decades at least.
GABRIEL: Numbers not being your strong point.

    Pause.

CASSIE: You haven't changed.
GABRIEL: That's biologically impossible.
CASSIE: Well, you were old when we met.
GABRIEL: Old but not wise.
CASSIE: You snuck in the back way?
GABRIEL: No, I came in the front entrance.
CASSIE: Bold.
GABRIEL: If you say so.
CASSIE: When I met the American President, they took me undercover.

GABRIEL: You must have been important back then.
CASSIE: They didn't want the generals from The Pentagon to see me. When generals wielding plutonium-dipped warheads came to the White House, they were as popular as ice-cream vans handing out chocolate-dipped swirly cones.
GABRIEL: Nowadays there are climate change activists visiting the President who advocate for nuclear power.
CASSIE: Because they are medically and scientifically illiterate.
GABRIEL: I suppose they have been 'taken in by pro-nuclear sociopaths who know no medicine and don't understand genetics'.
CASSIE: I'm still a member of International Physicians for the Prevention of Nuclear War.
GABRIEL: Is that still going? I think anti-nuclear is seen as a bit of a thing of the past.
CASSIE: It should be seen as one of the great achievements of the twentieth century. That we prevented proliferation.
GABRIEL: Ah, the eighties. I think I saw you on TV with an agent from Hollywood.
CASSIE: She got me *Vogue*, *Life*, *TIME*, *Ladies' Home Journal* and all the television shows. Donahue and Andy Griffiths and all of them. We had over eighty percent of Americans opposing nuclear weapons and supporting a nuclear weapons freeze, which wasn't good enough, but we were winning.
GABRIEL: And now?

Pause.

CASSIE: Now I hear you're on the advisory committee.
GABRIEL: I'm not taking meetings.
CASSIE: But you're part of the advocacy lobby.
GABRIEL: That's right.
CASSIE: I can imagine what you are telling them.
GABRIEL: I'm telling them that nuclear power does not lead to nuclear war.
CASSIE: Cleft palate, club feet, babies with six fingers and seven toes, children with fused fingers and toes, congenital heart disease, cerebrospinal fluid build-up, microcephaly, epilepsy.
GABRIEL: Alright.

CASSIE: Cerebral palsy, blindness, artificial lung ventilation.
GABRIEL: Alright.
CASSIE: Convulsive seizures.
GABRIEL: Nuclear power does not do that to children.
CASSIE: You're liars and charlatans and by the time the legacy of your decisions is visited on our grandchildren, you will be long dead. I worked to safeguard our children's future. I prevented nuclear war!
GABRIEL: And so they used fossil fuels and warmed the planet to the point where we can't live on it anymore.
CASSIE: That's not the point.
GABRIEL: The threat of nuclear disaster is miniscule compared to the certain apocalypse of continuing to use carbon, coal, oil and all the other things that our generations thrived on.
CASSIE: Brilliant. You should call it nice nuclear. Or how about ethical uranium. Or go the whole nine yards and just say fabulous fission.
GABRIEL: I could tell you why all your presumptions about the safety of nuclear power are wrong.
CASSIE: Unless you have found a way to change the radio isotopes of the waste Gabriel, unless you have made a discovery that will upend the periodic table and secure you a Nobel Prize for Science, you will never convince me.

Pause.

GABRIEL: So you've heard about Jervis Bay.
CASSIE: What about it?
GABRIEL: They've asked me to do a new risk assessment.
CASSIE: No.
GABRIEL: They have. It's back on the cards.
CASSIE: No, I mean. They can't do that.
GABRIEL: Says Cassie Logart?
CASSIE: They can't.
GABRIEL: They can ask me to consider it.
CASSIE: As a prospective site for a new nuclear power station.
GABRIEL: So you did know?
CASSIE: I know you condemned Hobart and Darwin to a similar fate. They're your preferred places for the nuclear subs to visit.

GABRIEL: I did those risk assessments.
CASSIE: I know.
GABRIEL: How do you know?
CASSIE: I know everything you ever did.

Pause.

GABRIEL: But how did you know, specifically, about Jervis Bay?
CASSIE: I didn't. You just told me.
GABRIEL: You made an educated guess.
CASSIE: I think that's the nicest thing you've ever said to me.
GABRIEL: Sorry.

Beat.

My mistake. I think I should go.
CASSIE: Wait. I have something for you.

She tears off her clothes and pulls a beta-ray protection suit on.

GABRIEL: What are you doing?
CASSIE: I want to show you my suit.
GABRIEL: Japanese.
CASSIE: Yes. It deflects one hundred percent of beta rays.
GABRIEL: I am well aware that the problem with radiation is not beta rays.
CASSIE: Or alpha rays.
GABRIEL: It's gamma rays.
CASSIE: Do any of the people who so quietly and shyly now say that nuclear is a viable option, talk about protection from gamma rays?
GABRIEL: No but this—
CASSIE: No. Because nothing can protect you from gamma rays except eighteen centimetres of lead or a metre thick of concrete. Certainly not this suit that they are pedalling in Japan to the survivors of the Fukushima nuclear accident.
GABRIEL: There will always be opportunists.
CASSIE: Won't there just. Always be unwanted feelings that come at you, seeping past your defences with long fingers of longing. Wounds that weep for the balm of touch.

She looks hard at GABRIEL.

GABRIEL: Beta particles are stopped by any form of heavy-duty clothing. You didn't need to get into this suit.

CASSIE: Made you look.

> *Pause.*

GABRIEL: Stop giving me information.
CASSIE: I need to tell you something.
GABRIEL: I'm not a journalist who needs information from you.
CASSIE: Then why are you here?
GABRIEL: I don't trust your information or your science.
CASSIE: Why did you come?
GABRIEL: And the media shouldn't either.
CASSIE: Why are you still looking?

> *Stops.*

GABRIEL: The woman on the phone used the word … executor.
CASSIE: Ah, that.
GABRIEL: For your will?
CASSIE: There's no-one else.
GABRIEL: I can't be your executor, Cassie.
CASSIE: It's quite simple, it's all just left to my daughter.
GABRIEL: Are you unwell?
CASSIE: One has to organise these things.
GABRIEL: I'm older than you, Cassie.
CASSIE: Then you'll likely never have to do it.
GABRIEL: There must be a friend, a colleague.
CASSIE: There isn't anyone I can trust.
GABRIEL: No.
CASSIE: Do this for me, Gabriel.
GABRIEL: No. Absolutely no.
CASSIE: Don't make me beg.
GABRIEL: Don't twist my arm.
CASSIE: I haven't told you something.

> *Pause. Suddenly* CASSIE *turns, trying to prevent herself from vomiting.*

GABRIEL: Nausea, vomiting, fatigue.
CASSIE: It's better when you mime them.
GABRIEL: Fainting, confusion.

> *He looks at her.*

CASSIE: I can't find a way to say it.

Pause.

I'm so scared.

GABRIEL *looks at her.*

You're a doctor, you can see the signs.
GABRIEL: I'm a Doctor of Engineering.
CASSIE: And the biological effects of ageing.

She swoons.

GABRIEL: Cassie, what's wrong?
CASSIE: I don't feel well.
GABRIEL: What is it?
CASSIE: It's the thing that takes you.
GABRIEL: Takes you where?
CASSIE: Nowhere I want to go.

Pause.

GABRIEL: Are you having treatment?
CASSIE: Yes.
GABRIEL: Radiation?
CASSIE: Yes.
GABRIEL: So much for Linear No-Threshold.
CASSIE: Fuck you.

Pause.

GABRIEL: I'm sorry this is happening to you.
CASSIE: I don't want to die bitter.
GABRIEL: And are you?
CASSIE: Terribly, terribly bitter. And not in the least reconciled to what happened, that one night, between us.
GABRIEL: You can't think about that now.
CASSIE: But I do. Most days.
GABRIEL: I really am sorry that this is happening to you.
CASSIE: Oh, please. Don't be nice to me. That's going to hasten me into my grave faster than a sunset stroll around Three Mile Island.
GABRIEL: What do you think, when you remember that night?
CASSIE: I should have destroyed you.

GABRIEL: Why didn't you?
CASSIE: You were an apologist for radiation poisoning.
GABRIEL: I still am.
CASSIE: I knew how to poison your world and I chose not to use it. Until now.
GABRIEL: You can't use it now.
CASSIE: Can't I?
GABRIEL: I think the shelf life on any scandal involving me and you has expired.
CASSIE: You expect me to sit around watching you increase the leukemia risk for every child living within five kilometres of a nuclear power station?
GABRIEL: Like you made me sit around and watch all the environmental damage done by fossil fuels? The species wiped out. We could have prevented that with nuclear power stations.
CASSIE: Liar!
GABRIEL: You're the liar, and the scaremonger.
CASSIE: How does all your fancy engineering prevent Nutty the Elf from blowing it up?
GABRIEL: Nuclear power produces more electricity on less land than any other source.
CASSIE: I have never been able to believe that an intelligent man cannot anticipate a world where regulation is not a priority for every regime in power.
GABRIEL: The only question. The only impediment is that there is a finite source of uranium.
CASSIE: Thirty-five million cases of cancer by 2050.
GABRIEL: Caused by obesity, ageing, lack of exercise.
CASSIE: And exposure to pollution.
GABRIEL: From coal. From plastic.
CASSIE: And from nuclear waste. I'm going to say publicly that there's a direct line from my illness to your advocacy. Our liaison is just the sort of colour it needs to go viral.

Pause.

GABRIEL: You're done. You're finished. There's nothing else you can do.

Pause.

CASSIE: My daughter Trudy.
GABRIEL: Is she tending pro?
CASSIE: What?
GABRIEL: Mine have joined the Greens so it's logical yours might go the other way. They say that growing up, it was like having Homer Simpson as a father.
CASSIE: So how do you resolve your differences with them?
GABRIEL: We don't talk about it.
CASSIE: You told your wife about that night.
GABRIEL: Yes.
CASSIE: Did you tell your children?
GABRIEL: No.

Pause.

CASSIE: And now you should ask if I told mine.

Pause.

GABRIEL: Does your daughter know how ill you are?
CASSIE: I don't think so.
GABRIEL: You have to tell her.
CASSIE: I want you to tell her.

Pause.

GABRIEL: Oh, I see. You want her to petition me about Jervis Bay. You want her to take up the cause that your mother gave to you. The family business.
CASSIE: The human business.

Pause.

GABRIEL: I'll come back. You can tell me then. I know where you are now. We can talk about the eighties. Reminisce.

Pause.

CASSIE: Before you go.
GABRIEL: I really have enjoyed seeing you.
CASSIE: Read to me. I can't see properly. Read to me.
GABRIEL: Sacred texts?
CASSIE: Hansard.
GABRIEL: You're kidding.

CASSIE: My idea of a party is the bear pit of Parliament.
I listen to Parliament on the radio every day it sits.
Who needs desert island discs when you can listen to Parliament? Who needs books when you've got Hansard?

She hands him the Hansard transcript, open to a particular page.

I prefer the ones who speak well, or can at least string a sentence together with a subject and a verb.
Then you can really scream at them.
Read to me.
GABRIEL: The hour I was crushed.
CASSIE: The hour you were cancelled.
GABRIEL: No.
CASSIE: You want to play?
GABRIEL: I don't.
CASSIE: Read Yellow Cake Bate for me.
GABRIEL: I won't.
CASSIE: The long game. The long game. Do you still want to play?
GABRIEL: [*reading*] 'Mr Jeff Bate. The Honourable Member for Macarthur. The Australian Labor Party is practically gloating over the fact that we are not going ahead with the construction of this nuclear power station at Jervis Bay.'
CASSIE: Hansard 1971. Transcript of the twenty-seventh Parliament of Australia.
GABRIEL: [*as Bate*] 'All the anti-pollutionists and all these other characters are getting on the band wagon … and we are getting the fallout from those demonstrations in here.'
CASSIE: That's us. He's talking about activists. There we are in the public record.
GABRIEL: [*as Bate*] 'They call it democracy.'
CASSIE: That's efficacy. That's legacy.
GABRIEL: [*as Bate*] 'It is an attack on progress and on Australia's need for power.'
CASSIE: Australia also needs fresh air to breathe, dingleberry.
GABRIEL: [*as Bate*] '… I urge the Government to go on with this nuclear power station; there is no escape from going on with it.'

She takes the Hansard transcript from him and closes it.

CASSIE: They didn't go on with it. We stopped it.
GABRIEL: That was fifty years ago.
CASSIE: We won.
GABRIEL: Past tense.
CASSIE: We won.
GABRIEL: Did win?
CASSIE: We won the argument.
GABRIEL: You delayed the inevitable.
CASSIE: We fought and we won.
GABRIEL: We can't get the energy we need from renewables.
CASSIE: It's ridiculously expensive.
GABRIEL: Nuclear is the only way to rapidly decarbonise.
CASSIE: We fought and we won.
GABRIEL: But the long game. The long game. Do you still want to play?
CASSIE: 'If you were dying, alone, I wouldn't spit on your grave.'
GABRIEL: Hey angry lady, stop making choices and then blaming me.

Pause.

CASSIE: One last happening.
GABRIEL: A sit in?
CASSIE: A reckoning.
GABRIEL: Where?
CASSIE: Out along the road to nowhere.
GABRIEL: Out on the Murrays Beach car park?

She takes a small butane chef's blowtorch out of her bag.

CASSIE: Go with me or I will aim this at my feet to show exactly what gamma rays do to human skin.

She turns the torch on.

GABRIEL: Cassie. Put it down.

The lights go down slowly so that only the hissing of the butane torch in the dark is visible and audible as CASSIE *speaks.*

CASSIE: Gamma rays do not burn with a flame that you can see, they burn like a clear acid, like a chemical reaction, like a hot blade on soft skin. They sting like fury, like the cough of the 'o' in 'inchoate' and the slice of the 'a' in 'rage'. The monster is never an option, never a solution, never an alternative. The monster is precisely a demon because it appears so simple, so reformable, so able to be rescued from the mire in which it has been discarded. Beware the day you wash it off and cover it with flowers. The monster is merciless, merciless, and masquerades as able to be controlled, like all desire does.

He tries to struggle with her to get the torch. She screams in pain.

8.

The lights come up and CASSIE *is outdoors, at Murrays Beach, standing in the centre of a large concrete platform. There is the sound of nature, the blue of the sky and the ocean. Her scream becomes the scream of a yellow-tailed black cockatoo.*

CASSIE: The trip out along the peninsula. Beautiful. Every tree a testament to what we fought for. Every limb and leaf, every bird and beetle and black-faced wallaby. The soil and the sand and the snakes. How it thrills me, thrills me to be going past every single little bit of nature wild and fecund and green.

With care she takes a long chain (which might be the long cord of her dressing gown) out of her bag and chains herself to a large tree.

He goes toward her.

Come any closer and I'll do it.

GABRIEL: Do what?

CASSIE: I've been down to the beach. I've scooped up a whole lot of bluebottles. Look.

She holds out a bowl full of bluebottles (which might be shampoo bottles).

GABRIEL: And what are you going to do with them?

CASSIE: I'll throw them at you. And they do sting.

GABRIEL: And then what?

CASSIE: And then I'll swallow them.

Pause.

GABRIEL: Where are you, Cassie?

CASSIE: Looking up into the lime green light of the forest. Her fist in the air, her breath on my cheek. In the place where she gave me my voice.

GABRIEL: Gave you frustration.

CASSIE: I can implicate you.

GABRIEL: In what?

CASSIE: Pro-nuclear scientist linked to death of anti-nuclear activist. Old feud turns toxic.

Pause.

GABRIEL: Cassie, please.

CASSIE: You can see where I am.

GABRIEL: Remind me what it's called.

CASSIE: Murrays Beach, where you are going to build the reactor. My mother brought me here all those years ago.

GABRIEL: Would you like to go out to Murrays, Cassie?

CASSIE: What do you mean? Oh, you think you'll confuse me and that will make me take off the chain?

GABRIEL: The chain?

CASSIE: I'm chained to this tree for a reason you know.

GABRIEL: I don't know.

CASSIE: You can hang from a chain as well as from a rope.

GABRIEL: You're hallucinating, Cassie. It's the medication.

CASSIE: As long as you're with me it will work.

GABRIEL: What will work?

CASSIE: Executor, executioner.

GABRIEL: Cassie I know you're not mad. And I know you're not serious.

Beat.

So what are you playing at?

CASSIE: Tell me what you see?

GABRIEL: What I see?

CASSIE: You come down your road to nowhere …

GABRIEL: I slow to forty, for the wildlife.

CASSIE: You see a large, cleared area, a football field, an oval of earth.

GABRIEL: The footing of the reactor. The concrete foundations.

CASSIE: You want to muffle fairyland.

GABRIEL: I see a space to build. An emptiness to fill.

CASSIE: I see a hole torn in rapture.
GABRIEL: I see a car park with access to the beach.
CASSIE: I see the Elysian Fields with a gravel rash.
GABRIEL: We turned the ocean outflow into a boat ramp.

Pause.

CASSIE: We came so close.
GABRIEL: We came so close.

Pause.

How about you quit with the clickbait theatrics, Cassie.
CASSIE: I will do whatever it takes.
GABRIEL: Look around, there is no-one here to document your photogenic performance.
CASSIE: I can post that I was blackmailing you. So you chained me to a tree and left me. Exposure. It doesn't even have to be true. It just has to inflame the tribes.
GABRIEL: I think you're overestimating how much anyone should care about one night all those years ago.
CASSIE: I have to tell you something.
GABRIEL: Say it.
CASSIE: [*cries out*] I have to tell you something.
GABRIEL: Just tell me.
CASSIE: [*screams*] I can't.
GABRIEL: What happens when you try to tell me?

Pause.

CASSIE: Shame.
GABRIEL: For what?
CASSIE: The lie.

GABRIEL *lets out a high-pitched cry, like a black cockatoo.*

Yellow boys.
Yellow-tail black cockatoos.
She calls them yellow boys.
GABRIEL: Who?
CASSIE: Trudy.
GABRIEL: Trudy, our daughter?

Stops.

CASSIE: She loves how they flap their wings so slow.
GABRIEL: I saw a photo of you with her.
CASSIE: Calling as they fly.
GABRIEL: She looks like me.
CASSIE: She says that's how you can tell they aren't ravens.
GABRIEL: That's when I knew.

Pause.

CASSIE: You knew.
GABRIEL: Yes.
CASSIE: And when I bumped into you at the pool?
GABRIEL: Yes.
CASSIE: You knew then?

GABRIEL nods. She removes the chain from herself.

You were so angry and I thought, well I don't know him but that's a lot of anger.

Beat.

But you knew?
GABRIEL: Yes.

Pause.

CASSIE: You never said.
GABRIEL: Neither did you.

Pause.

I saw you once, in IKEA. One of those maze stores where you go in and then you have to walk through the entire store to get out.
CASSIE: And you get lost and go round in circles.
GABRIEL: A maze is not really a circle.
CASSIE: I liked their stationery. The patterns on their magazine holders.
GABRIEL: That will date you.
CASSIE: But when you say 'saw you'. Do you mean, saw me or saw me and …
GABRIEL: Trudy. Short for Gertrude. Meaning 'sword'.
CASSIE: You should have come up and said hello.
GABRIEL: Don't say things you don't mean.
CASSIE: How could you not?

Pause.

GABRIEL: It wasn't a decision.

CASSIE: But it was.

GABRIEL: It was an indecision. I didn't see you, then when I did, I didn't say hello. And then it became an impasse. A stalemate. It was a neglect that became a habit. It just got too hard. Too complicated.

CASSIE: You were a coward.

GABRIEL: If I was, then so were you.

CASSIE: I asked you to come here.

GABRIEL: And I came as soon as you did.

CASSIE: I knew that I had to tell you.

GABRIEL: I respected your decision not to tell me. Not to include me in her life. Not to ever know her. You set the rules of the game.

CASSIE: You could have stood up to me.

GABRIEL: You are inflexible.

CASSIE: You could have convinced me to let you see her. However messy it was. You were too scared to challenge me.

GABRIEL: I came here.

CASSIE: You don't know how to change.

GABRIEL: I came here. I came to see you. I came. After thirty years, because I am good with numbers. I came here. A seismic shift. The tectonic plates spinning like an Easter Show ride. I am here. Here. I am looking you in the face. And I am so ashamed of everything that I have not done, that I have not said.

Pause.

You broke my heart.

CASSIE: You captured mine and never let it go.

GABRIEL *shakes his head.*

GABRIEL: What kind of future have we left her?

CASSIE: One where she can still hear yellow cockatoos at Jervis Bay.

GABRIEL: You had nothing to do with stopping the Jervis Bay reactor.

CASSIE: Not past tense, Gabriel.

GABRIEL: What do you mean?

CASSIE: Will you agree to be my executor?

GABRIEL: You're leaving everything to Trudy?

CASSIE: Yes.

    GABRIEL *nods.*

Say it please.

GABRIEL: Yes, I will be your executor.

CASSIE: One of the conditions of my will is that you will say that in your expert opinion Jervis Bay should never be considered ever again.

GABRIEL: Funny.

CASSIE: The executor's primary responsibility is to carry out the wishes of the deceased as stated in their will.

GABRIEL: You don't own my opinion.

CASSIE: You handed it back. It is jointly managed territory.

GABRIEL: Yes, of course it is.

CASSIE: I have appointed an executor who has it within his power to say that in his expert opinion, Jervis Bay should never again be considered ever. For me, for my mother, for our daughter.

    He looks at her.

Promise me.

GABRIEL: I will promise you … that in assessing the risk, I will take into account the ways in which the site has changed in the years since our initial assessment.

CASSIE: So what does that mean?

GABRIEL: That means there may be factors to consider that were not relevant at the time.

CASSIE: Like what?

GABRIEL: I don't know yet. I haven't begun the assessment. But it will include the fact that it is now jointly managed territory.

CASSIE: Promise me that you will protect it.

GABRIEL: I will promise you that all stakeholders will be given a chance to feed responses into the assessment.

    Pause.

CASSIE: It's not enough.

GABRIEL: It has to be enough. Or I will recuse myself.

CASSIE: You're saying no to me?

GABRIEL: I'm saying I won't do it because you put it in your will.

Pause.

GABRIEL: She calls them yellow boys?

But CASSIE *is silent.*

CASSIE: I'm cold.

GABRIEL *moves over to her.*

GABRIEL: Tell me how to look in a different way.

CASSIE: Use all of your senses.

GABRIEL: Like you did. When you were sitting at the top of a tree or camping on an old growth forest site?

CASSIE: I am a lobbyist, so I do less front-line action.

GABRIEL: So you don't put your body on the line in the same way?

CASSIE: Well I did.

Pause.

GABRIEL: What did you talk about?

CASSIE: We named things.

GABRIEL: Named things?

CASSIE: Like the winds. The wind that came up in the afternoon that was gusty, we named that Surly. The wind that was there in the morning but so quiet and gentle you could hardly notice it was there we named that Hope.

GABRIEL: Hiding in plain sight.

CASSIE: The wind that came before rain, the wind that formed into little whirlwinds, the wind that blew up your trousers and your nose, the chill wind, the whistling wind. We gave them different names.

GABRIEL: Like what?

CASSIE: I can't remember them all. I remember that someone called a westerly wind Wendy, and we all howled and said that you couldn't name a wind Wendy because it was so much like Windy and he said that was even more reason to call it Wendy and we all laughed and held hands against the storms of doubt swirling inside us.

GABRIEL: You against the world.

CASSIE: I called a wind Sweetness because it carried the smells of the forest, of pine and dirt and eucalyptus crushed into muddy oil.

GABRIEL: I know that smell. When we were clearing the trees for the road out to the reactor.

CASSIE: The sap escaping from the hacked-off trunks.
GABRIEL: Bury the hatchet.
CASSIE: Not funny.
GABRIEL: A bit funny.
CASSIE: Will you do something for me?
GABRIEL: What?
CASSIE: Get a photo. On your phone.

> GABRIEL *stands back. He shakes his head and puts his coat around her.*
>
> *She sits shivering. He takes a photo of her.*

You'll give it to the papers?
GABRIEL: They're all online now, Cassie.
I can put it up on my Instagram account.
The vision-impaired image description will say, 'A beautiful lady is chained to a tree in a car park. Go figure.'
CASSIE: The image descriptions do not say 'go figure'.
GABRIEL: They should.
CASSIE: Next you'll want a star rating.
GABRIEL: Isn't that just the number of likes?
CASSIE: I can still out-like you any day, Gabriel.
GABRIEL: Yeah, well, I've never chained myself to a tree.

> *Pause. He takes a photo of the two of them, together.*

CASSIE: When I'm dead … how are you going to explain going to my funeral to your pro-nuclear mates?
GABRIEL: I won't need to explain, I'll have a photo.
CASSIE: But you will go to my funeral?
GABRIEL: I guess that's where I'll be meeting our daughter.
CASSIE: She is our daughter. And when she meets you she's going to have questions.
GABRIEL: Of course.
CASSIE: When she knows the whole story, what we did, why I went to that bar … she's going to think that's why I lied to her. She's going to think I was ashamed of who you are, what you believe.
GABRIEL: You hate what I believe.
CASSIE: I need her to know that I never regretted that she came from you.

GABRIEL: Then just tell her that.

CASSIE: You can't tell someone that. You have to show her that. Listen to her. Argue with her. The whole 'not simple, not easy, no slogans' truth about the man I loved. Have always loved. Do love.

He looks at her and nods.

GABRIEL: I'll tell her she was conceived in a blaze of joy.

She smiles.

CASSIE: Now send the photo of us to all your pro-nuclear followers. To give them a laugh.

GABRIEL: Or I can text it to you and you can send it on to your anti-nuke buddies in the movement. Or what's left of it.

CASSIE: You're wrong. There is a movement still, and it's strong too. Because it's right.

Pause.

It's. Just. Not you.

GABRIEL: I've wasted so much time—

CASSIE: I've wasted so much time—

GABRIEL: Hoping—

CASSIE: and wishing—

GABRIEL: and arguing—

CASSIE: There are still people of all ages who want change—

GABRIEL: and will work for change—

CASSIE: We will defeat you again and again and again.

GABRIEL: For too long—

CASSIE: For so long, I wanted you to be something else—

GABRIEL: I wanted you to be someone else—

CASSIE: But you can only be you—

GABRIEL: And you can only be you.

They look at each other, as if for the first time.

There is the plaintive sound of a black cockatoo.

We can agree on this, Cassie. The future is in their hands, not ours, the decisions you have made will be changed. And then so will mine.

CASSIE: We will leave our grandchildren with impossible pollution and deformity.

GABRIEL: We made our choices.
CASSIE: We did. We made proud choices.
GABRIEL: Wrap yourself around your tree.

> *He gets up and takes the photo. He looks down at it as* CASSIE *dies.*

Now shall we do one with you standing? Cassie—

> *He goes over to her. He realises that she is dead.*
>
> *He holds her like a pietà, dead in his arms.*
>
> *He cries.*
>
> *Lights fade.*

THE END

www.ingramcontent.com/pod-product-compliance
Lightning Source LLC
Chambersburg PA
CBHW050027090426
42734CB00021B/3452